A Nest
in the Heart

A Nest
in the Heart

❧

Vivienne Popperl

A Publication of The Poetry Box®

Editing & Book Design by Shawn Aveningo Sanders
Cover Design by Robert R. Sanders
Author Photo by Franz Popperl

ISBN: 978-1-948461-99-3
Library of Congress Control Number: 2021921429
Printed in the United States of America.
Wholesale Distribution via Ingram.

Published by The Poetry Box®, April 2022
Portland, Oregon
ThePoetryBox.com

for Saskia

I was profoundly influenced by the poetry of Elizabeth Woody which emanates a deep sense of place. It prompted me to ask, where is my body's landscape? Where does my physical body belong in the natural, geographical world? This collection is an attempt to start to answer that question for myself and my family.

Contents

TO THOSE WHO CAME BEFORE ME

To Those Who Came Before Me — 13

WORDS FROM MY MOTHER'S HEADSTONE

Early Spring 1913, Roskiskis, Lithuania — 17

Winter 1919, Lithuania — 20

First Winter in Kopjes, South Africa — 22

South Africa, 1925: A Refugee from Lithuania Reflects on Her New Life — 23

Conversing with My Mother's Father in the Afterworld — 24

Rain in Kopjes — 25

My Mother Remembers Learning Piano, Kopjes, South Africa 1925 — 26

The Art of Medicine — 28

Devotional — 29

Johannesburg Diamond — 30

Deschutes River Dream — 31

WORDS FROM MY FATHER'S HEADSTONE

What She Told Her Family about Her New Life — 35

Descendants — 37

My Father — 39

Winter Dream — 40

Dad & Ezra & the Cold War — 42

The Daily Newspaper Circa 1960,
    Johannesburg, South Africa   43

Ritual   44

Yorzeit   46

FROM JOHANNESBURG CHILDHOOD TO OREGON

Summer 1957, Johannesburg, South Africa   49

Black and White in Johannesburg   50

Inyanga   53

Emma Mends the World   55

Flip Side   56

Aunty Ruby's Eyes   58

Hitch, or My Summer of Love   59

Johannesburg   60

The Girl Who Raised Fantail Pigeons   62

Tomatoes   63

"I'll Blame It on the Wind"   65

Land and Body   67

After "The Other Hours" by Li-Young Lee   69

❧

Notes   73

Acknowledgments   75

In Gratitude   77

Praise for *A Nest in the Heart*   79

About the Author   81

About The Poetry Box®   83

A Nest
in the Heart

TO THOSE WHO CAME BEFORE ME

"Trees have roots. Jews have legs.
Displacement is hard.
A new land is also the loss of the old."

—Roger Cohen,
New York Times, 11/15/2020

To Those Who Came Before Me

Ninety percent of my cells, they have discovered
are not my own person,
they are other beings inside me

      —Jane Hirshfeld, "My Proteins"

Even crossing one sea, one ocean and three continents
could not lose them.
They stowed away snug within me,
grandmothers whose names I bear,
grandfathers I know only from stories.

I am Musha, dark eyes, dark hair, thin lips, black garb.
I am Chaya, soft spoken, shy, a small swirling gold brooch
pinned over my heart, a bouquet of flowers in my arms.

I am Avram Lippman, lover of books and conversation,
afraid of failure, always a stranger in a foreign land.
I am Moishe, adventurer, provider, practical.

I smell mothballs, lavender, pipe tobacco,
weak black tea with lemon. I taste pickled herring,
chopped liver with hard-boiled egg,
kichlach, and kreplach.

I find a corner in Laurelhurst Park,
build a picnic of crunchy baguette,
creamy chevre, sliced tangy tomatoes,
olive oil, balsamic vinegar, basil.

Before I bite off a mouthful I make an offering.
Oh you who came before me, you who are within me
will you accept my gift?

FROM MY MOTHER'S HEADSTONE

"And Therefore, Choose Life"
Uvecharta bachaim
—Deuteronomy, Ch. 30 v. 19

Avraham m. Sorah

Noach Zvi m. Miriam

Morris m. Chaya

Mathilda, my mother

Early Spring 1913

Footsteps creak back and forth
across the wooden floor.
My daughter paces.
She clutches her baby, Matla, in her arms,
gently presses her lips
to flushed cheeks, dank forehead.

The infant's breath catches, rasps.
She whimpers, coughs.
Wind shakes the small house.

Why isn't she getting better?
It's been two days. She's not nursing.
My daughter's voice trembles. *I feel the breath*
of the Angel of Death.

I find my husband.
He shakes his head, *no.*
My voice cracks. *Please!*

Two hours later ten men
shuffle in, prayer books in hand. They surround
the young mother, avert their eyes. They begin to pray.
May the one who blessed our forefathers
and foremothers...
The hum of familiar Hebrew words
fills the gloom.

My daughter stands silent, her eyes
search the faces of the praying men.

[. . .]

What name? my husband asks.
What? She stares, shakes her head.

Sorah, your grand-mother's name,
I hear myself say.

Now in the presence of loved ones
we give you the name 'Sorah'...
The low mutter of Hebrew words resumes.

The men finish the prayer,
duck their heads
beneath the low door frame,
file out.
Their black coats
melt into midnight dark.

I add wood to the fire.
My daughter rocks the baby.
I hear her whisper,
Sorah, Sorahleh.

I settle into a corner.
Wind rattles the glass panes.
I feel the air move. Out of the corner
of my eye I see a wide shadow swoop,
darken the window
hover
swerve.

Early light fills the room,
touches the baby, the mother.

They gaze into each other's eyes.
Sorah's pursed lips
sound quiet chirps.
She drinks.

Winter 1919, Lithuania

I smile
I arch my brows
I glance side-long
I swing my hips
I twirl
I place my hands at my waist

I see the soldier stop raking
the fireplace with his rifle
I see him push his cap to the back of his head
sling his rifle over his shoulder
extract tobacco and thin white papers
from an inside pocket
lick his lips
before his pink tongue seals the cigarette shut

I see him grin
watch me slip my thumbs
inside my waistband
over the elastic of my mother's flannel bloomers
beneath my wide skirt
tap my feet, click my heels
to mask the faint clack of silver knives, forks, spoons,
two candle sticks wrapped in a soft white cloth
snug inside my mother's bloomers
under my wide petticoats

I burst into song
we sing in the sun as we plough the black earth
I clap, yodel
the soldier joins in, conducts,
cigarette between index finger and thumb
smoke and shards of tobacco scatter

he throws the cigarette butt on the rug
we watch a black hole slowly widen
he stares at each of us
purses his lips
spits
walks out

I keep singing
my mother, back to the wall, waits
two more verses
she stamps out the embers on the rug
turns her pale face to me
I reach under my skirt
pull off the baggy flannel bloomers
wrap them around their silver burden
hand them to her
singing

First Winter in Kopjes, South Africa

We smell winter arrive in smoky trails of wind
lurking low over dry fields.
Grey dust fills our mouths and eyes.

I knit hats for the children,
pull them low over their ears each morning.

They always come home bare-headed.
They itch, Mama, and we can't hear our friends
 count to 100 when we hide in the ditch.

Daytime sunshine lulls us
into shucking our coats.

Sunset winds surprise us
with tremolo blasts of cold.

Evenings blaze orange and red
against a black-blue sky.

Winter nights are so dark.
Stars pierce the sky with light
as white as icicles hanging
off the roof of our old house
in Lithuania.

South Africa, 1925:
A Refugee from Lithuania
Reflects on Her New Life

It was hard at the shop. I couldn't really speak
English or Afrikaans. Maurice tried to teach me.

The children tried to teach me. *Say 'good morning,'*
not 'gut morgan.' They laughed and ran away.

I understood the quiet pointing and gestures of black
people better. *Eh?* they pointed. *How much?*

I would hold up three fingers, put the bottle of cooking
oil in a basket, nod my head to take a bag of cornmeal.

They slipped their battered pennies into my hand. My finger tips
brushed their calloused palms. We lowered our heads to each other.

Sometimes I included a few boiled sweets with the change,
smiled at ragged children clutching skirts,

bright-eyed babies tucked tightly on their mother's
backs. The steely blue stare of the white Afrikaner

farmer's wife pulled me back behind the counter.
Gut morgan, palms flat on the polished wooden surface,
I leaned forward, smiled.

Conversing with My Mother's Father
in the Afterworld

I know some Yiddish.
He knows some English.

We both know the sound
of a kettle boiling.

I offer my grandfather lemons
and strawberry jam for his tea.

He chooses a sugar cube
holds it between his teeth
sucks his tea through the sweet strainer.

I tell him chocolate. I tell him mint.

Somewhere in his old country snow is falling.
Somewhere in his old country heavy black shoes
trudge through deep snow.

I tell him green. I tell him puddles. I tell him rain.
I tell him matted leaves, loam.
I tell him mud. I tell him Douglas fir,
hemlock, spruce, pine.

He tells me honor. He tells me security.
He tells me hard work. He tells me gentleness.

He tells me twenty years growing corn
on the flat dusty African plain
were the happiest of his life.

Rain In Kopjes

Rain in Kopjes was rare
Dusty paths and riverbeds turned to mud
Mathilda roamed freely, feet bare
Squelched the ooze between her toes, hidden in mud

Dusty paths and riverbeds turned to mud
Little brother Peter hunted frogs in ditches
Squelched the ooze between his toes, hidden in mud
Lay on his belly, arms shoulder deep in wet brown ditches

Little brother Peter hunted frogs in ditches
Mathilda roamed freely, feet bare
Peter lay on his belly, arms shoulder deep in wet brown ditches
Rain in Kopjes was rare

My Mother Remembers Learning Piano

Kopjes, South Africa 1925

Miss E. Bell-Robinson stands behind white lace curtains.
Her fingers circle a cut-glass goblet. An amber liquid glints.

She watches as I push through the garden gate.
She sips as I reach up, lift and drop the brass door knocker.

The thick oak door swings open.
I blink in the sunless room, inhale the nutty, smoky aroma.
Bottles of Irish whisky line a mahogany shelf.

Miss E. Bell-Robinson sets the goblet on the piano,
leans over, presses her long fingers over mine on the keys.
Straitch, straitch to th' octave!
'ave you bin practicin'? Spread yer fingers!

When we play a duet, her lips
curl slightly up.

The kids in my school spit. *Ole spinster!*
They poke me in the ribs. They yell,
ole Bell-Robinson's panties fell down!
They nearly hit the groun'! She picked 'em up, stuffed 'em
in a pocket in her gown! Drunken ole witch!

I twist away, clutch my music book.
You don't know her! I shout.

I'd seen the glossy, black and white photo,
the smiling pianist, her long fingers poised over the keys,
her black dress tight and smooth. I'd seen the certificate,
First Prize for Piano Forte, the gold seal.

I still sometimes play piano,
close my eyes,
let the cascade of notes
flow over me,
smell the nutty, smoky aroma,
hear Miss E. Bell Robinson's Irish brogue
see her lips
curl slightly up.

The Art of Medicine

she listened for the unseen
read the signs and sounds
above and beneath the skin

she gathered up her tall frame
trained her serious brown eyes
on yours

she reached her cool hand to your brow
a slight pressure, gathering data,
its heat, its moisture

her grasp on your wrist
firm but gentle
her gaze toward the little watch

pinned upside down on her blouse
time upside down
but not to her

she focused within, stethoscope to her ears
listened
your heart, your lungs, your stomach

she set boundaries
fenced off pain and illness
freed your body to heal itself

Devotional

~after Lisel Mueller

the words *start over again*
held no terror for her

the wide brown eyes of her five-year-old self
saw cattle cars and snow, steamships and oceans
the full moon over Table Mountain

she fixed her steady gaze on medical school in Johannesburg
left the safety and love of her parents' home
in the dusty town

she kept her nerve as a widow
crossed continents and oceans
brought with her the nest she stowed in her heart

she walked in the snow in Cleveland
pressed her stick down firmly to the sidewalk
reached for bedrock with every step

Johannesburg Diamond

My parents went to the diamond dealer together before they married.
My mother wore the diamond ring for the rest of her life.

When she kneaded sweet yeast dough for cinnamon bulkes
her ringed knuckle left facets impressed in the unbaked rolls.

When she treated patients in the hospital she turned the ring around.
The diamond faced the inside of her hand, protected by her palm.

When she gardened, the reddish soil slipped inside her gloves.
She rubbed the ring clean with a soft toothbrush.

Once she cut herself on the edge of a can of pears.
The jeweler cut the white-gold band off her swollen finger.

When she was in the hospital during her last year
nurses secured the ring to her finger with paper-thin medical tape.

After she died I kept the ring locked in a safe deposit box.
For fifteen years it lay in the rectangular metal dark.

When my daughter and her love got engaged I gave the ring to them.
Now the diamond crowns my daughter's left hand, refracts light.

Deschutes River Dream

The river is green opaque, swift.
Current runs steady, deep.

Reeds sway at river's edge.
Hooded Mergansers rustle,

break free. Tree-swallows cut the sky
into blue scraps above yellow kayaks.

An osprey folds black wings,
plummets head down into glassy depths,

emerges, a line of silver between its talons.
We three bicyclists roll down the path

beside the river. Sunshine glints, blinds.
We turn to cross the wooden bridge.

Tires thud, bump across each join between planks.
We stop, look back along the river.

A woman appears among the Ponderosa pines.
Tendrils of grey hair escape her green straw hat,

a scarf threaded tightly through the brim,
knotted below her chin. I recognize her upright stance,

her direct glance. My mother stands poised at an easel,
slim black paintbrush between her fingers.

For a long minute she stares at us.
Then she is gone.

[. . .]

When I awake I search for the painting.
There's the bridge arching over the green river.

There are the three cyclists. There, the brown dog.
There, always, the blue sky.

FROM MY FATHER'S HEADSTONE

"His hands remained an expression of trust
until the sun set."
Vayehi yadav emuna ad bo hashachar.
—Exodus, chapter 17, v.12.

Avram Lipman m. Musa

Isaac, my father

What She Told Her Family about Her New Life

~after Li-Young Lee's "A Dove! I Said"

A rose, she said.
What she meant was a thicket.
What she meant was dusty earth.

A mountain blue-bird, she said.
What she meant was a store-room's barred windows.
What she meant was shelves of canned goods, sacks of flour.

A wide green meadow, she said.
What she meant was the smell of carbolic soap.
What she meant was scratching ciphers on a yellowed page.

A gold ring, she said.
What she meant was raw knuckles.
What she meant was chapped lips.

A cradle, she said.
What she meant was a kitchen table.
What she meant was a midwife between her legs.

Tiny silk stitches, she said.
What she meant was a goat cart to carry her children to school.
What she meant was a shotgun to defend them.

Blue silk and feathers, she said.
What she meant was a widow's black gabardine.
What she meant was a twisted rope.

Fire, she said.
What she meant was curled fingers poking through woolen gloves.
What she meant was hands smudged by coal.

[. . .]

*Fire, red flush of shame
heart burnt by grief;
Fire's single flame slants in the darkened doorway.*

*Fire lights the belly,
scours the heart.
Fire flares, spends itself in ashes.*

What she should have said was:
flames of bitterness.

What I want to say to her is:
*fierce brave heart left behind
you arose from the ashes.*

Descendants

-after Ocean Vuong's "Seventh Circle of Earth"

1

2

3

4

5

---

1 Avram, don't be afraid- don't do it, please./ Don't be ashamed of
your life. It is not a failure.

2 Think of your six children—the oldest is 16. The youngest is only
two. And your only daughter is ten years old./ She feels like you
are her only friend in this house of boys./ Even her mother loves
her sons more than her.

3 Avram, can you hear me?/ Put down that rope./ Get off that
chair./ Please, Avram./ Your children need you.

4 Avram, don't worry so much about money. Together with your
wife, you can find a way/ to feed your family./ Your wife needs
you, Avram.

5 Don't despair, Avram. Don't be afraid of life. Ignore the
accusation/ in your wife's black eyes.

[. . .]

6

7

8

9

---

6 Look, here's my father, your second son. He's fourteen./ He
   worships you. See how he sits in corners listening/ as you and
   your friends talk of books and ideas and literature./ See how he
   can't stop reading/ the volumes you gave him for his birthday.
7 Oh, Avram, don't do it./ Your action will reverberate/ in the lives
   of your wife, children and grandchildren./ If only you could see
   into the future,/ see the consequences.
8 See how your wife keeps a cow in the back yard to sell milk/
   and feed the children./ See how she takes in lodgers/ and does
   laundry/ and piece work sewing.
9 See your second son, how hungry and ashamed he is./ How
   grateful that his best friend buys him a sticky bun for lunch.

My Father

~after William Stafford's "Listening"

My father drove a turquoise, chrome-finned Buick.
He wore a suit and tie and fedora five days a week.

My father turned our back-seat squabbles into silly songs.
He spun limericks out of starlings with engagement rings.
chortled about guinea fowl strolling slowly abreast,
wings behind their backs like old men
walking home after services, heads bowed.

My father kept us holding our breath,
swallowing our guffaws, waiting for his resonant voice
to fill the car with more side-splitting doggerel.

My father relished words. At dinner he served up discussion
while my mother ladled chicken soup and filled plates with roast.

My father kept a carved wooden box on his desk,
empty except for a paper clip and the aroma of cherry tobacco.

My father sat in a dark room under a circle of light.
He turned each word in a contract this way and that
then dropped it into a sentence or excised it.

My father savored the *mot juste.*
Let me tell you.

Winter Dream

What flows out of my dreams
to meet me on the other side
of night?

What voices do I hear
from another room? From
another tomb?

Are they muffled by red brick
walls? Are they electronic TV
voices setting the plaster
on edge?

What is the title
winter knows me by?

Is it *Shivering*? Is it
Taking Small Steps Over Ice?
Is it *Blinking At The Sun's
Muted Eye*?

What was in the letter
my father never wrote?

Was it *my girl, you
broke my heart*? Was it
*my girl, why didn't you marry
a man who could take care of you*?

Was it *my girl*
I am proud of you?
I love you?

What was in the letter
I never wrote back?

Dad & Ezra & the Cold War

The first time we went to the Kruger National Park,
we joined Ezra's family.

Ezra was Dad's childhood friend.

We caravanned around to find wild animals to photograph
with our Brownie cameras.

We were allowed to switch cars if we wanted to.

It felt strange to ride in a car with someone else's parents,
guzzle salty snacks. We giggled in the trunk of Ezra's station wagon,
rolled around on our backs.

Dad and Ezra stopped often to confer about directions
and where to find more animals.

They stood outside the cars,
pointed up, pointed down, pointed horizontally,
told a running joke which left them dissolved in laughter
tears running down their cheeks.

What did Dad mean when he climbed into the car,
dried his tears with the back of his hand, said,
over here, you forget everything going on in the outside world.
You don't even think about the Congo.

The Daily Newspaper Circa 1960

Johannesburg, South Africa

Twice a day we welcomed you,
proud to be a two-paper-a-day family.

Rand Daily Mail in the morning
liberal, critical, satirical, risqué.
Dad read you first at breakfast
after his morning swim.

He left you bent half-open
and folded over at the story
that caught his eye.

When you reached our hands,
you smelled lightly of chlorine and soap.
You bore spots of tea, butter, and honey.

The Star, evening paper
was conventional, conservative.
When it arrived we flipped the tall pages to the political cartoons,
tried to fathom the stories behind the sketches.

Before Dad came home from work
we folded you back into your original neat shape, matched the creases,
smoothed the damp holes in the front page
from the teeth of the golden cocker-spaniel
who failed the day's lesson of how to pick you up.

We tried to forget gritty black-and-white photographs
of slim black children in grey v-necked sweaters
running from police
eyes uncertain.

Ritual

My sister says she remembers
seeing our grandfather
recite his morning prayers.

She sat in the low, blue velvet armchair
swinging her short legs.
She stared up at him
as he swayed
back and forth,
his lips opening and closing
releasing scratchy whispers
into the early morning sunshine.

I think I saw my brother pray.
Or maybe it's a photo I remember.
He wound black leather straps
around his left arm and across his forehead
so that the little black boxes
containing the special Hebrew words
were tied close to his heart
and as *frontlets* between his eyes.

I didn't know what *frontlets* were
until I searched in the dictionary:
A decorative band or ornament
worn on the forehead.

Girls could mouth the words
but never bind them next to their hearts
with soft leather
or as *frontlets* between their eyes.

Maybe that's why my father,
his voice icy quiet,
ordered me to remove
the narrow ribbon
patterned with flowers
twisted around my forehead,
holding down my dark curly hair.

Yorzeit

It's my father's *Yorzeit,*
anniversary of his death
according to the Jewish lunar calendar.

In three houses spaced across this continent
my siblings and I light special candles,
wax in a glass, remembrance.

We swap stories, questions, tears,
sometimes laughter, remember
how we kept vigil at his bedside.
How the night before he died
he sat up and said
I can only take you this far.

When I was little he swung me up
and settled me on his shoulders.
I remember his warm hands holding my ankles,
the smell of Vitalis as I wrapped my arms
around his forehead.

I remember the wind in my curls,
how different the world looked from my high perch
scary, yet how safe,
the sure swing of his gait moving forward.

Dad, I whisper, *you carried us
over continents
for decades.
You still do.*

FROM JOHANNESBURG CHILDHOOD TO OREGON:

Coming to Consciousness of Apartheid

Travel in Europe

Finding Home in Oregon

Summer 1957

Johannesburg, South Africa

in the yard of a child
a screen of sweet-peas
protects the princess
behind curling tendrils
ready to snap closed
on the wrist of any intruder

in the yard of a child
the princess lies on her belly
rubs sand stones to gold dust
trails fingers among purple Jacaranda flowers
on the swimming-pool surface

she smoothes and stacks the silky bells onto her finger tips
points, beckons, casts spells
tucks soft bruised petals
into old cigar boxes under the laurel hedge

in the yard of a child
the lawn swells with tufted hillocks

the princess roley-poleys downhill
dried grasses cling to her hair
fly into her laughing mouth

in the yard of a child
giant Deodar trees keep watch over a high stone wall
feathery branches wave off intruders

Black and White in Johannesburg

Emma's door
half-open
reveals cool darkness

I follow scents of paraffin,
beeswax, and Pond's face cream
into her room

Emma's iron bedstead looms
along one white-washed wall
two red bricks

under each leg
lift the bed
mattress to my shoulder level

keep Emma safe
from the Tokolosh
an evil spirit, always lurking

white sheets gleam
stitched in scallops and flowers
greens, pinks, reds

a bud vase balances
beside a miniature tree statue,
shiny gold picture frames

hold photos of people I do not know,
green and yellow bead necklaces
loop beside them

come in
I jump at the sound
of Emma's voice

you want to see a picture of my son?

we sit on the threshold of her room
stretch our bare legs
over the tarmac

into the winter sunshine
my pink, chubby feet
level with her soft brown knees

we admire the blurred
black and white photo
of her five-year-old boy

his white shirt and shorts gleam
his rectangular cardboard school bag
casts a shadow

his small hand disappears
in the clasp of a tall
black woman

my mother is taking him to school
Emma strokes the small picture
with her right thumb

he is in same class
like you

[. . .]

he is two
hundred miles
away

we sit together
quietly
in the sun

Inyanga

I remember you, *Inyanga*
reading bones.

Your last name was *Madiwa.*
But we, even the little children, called you *Dennis.*

You were tall. Your voice was deep, gruff,
your skull shaved smooth with a piece of glass.

In the morning you kneeled, brush in hand
on the long carpet in the narrow corridor.

You inched your way forward, smoothly swept the carpet
with a single swipe to each side.

You rolled up the carpet, thumped it into a corner.
You swept and polished the bare strip of dark wooden floor.

In the evening you made Machau and Umquembothi.
When you drank too much you fell down. You sat

head lowered, shaking, shaking
from side to side.

On your days off you climbed the dry rocky koppie
to gather plants and roots.

You mashed them into salves and bitter tonics,
boiled them in a battered tin can, sour steam rising.

On Sunday afternoons, lines of your patients
walked up the driveway to you, *Inyanga.*

[. . .]

You sat on a box, wrapped in an old coat,
a black hat on your head.

Your patient sat opposite, watched you
unwrap dried animal bones, carved bits of wood, shells,

throw them into the dust three times, point.
Your voice rumbled soft.

You stood, reached for a small vial,
pressed it into grateful hands.

After the last patient left, you carefully rewrapped talismans,
vials, roots, took off your coat, your hat.

You, *Dennis*, walked to the coal pile
loaded a bucket, fired up the pot-bellied, cast-iron stove

heated water for our evening baths.

Emma Mends the World

Her fingers coax the old light bulb
into the woolen sock.
She slides it up to the hole in the toe,
positions the bulge to stretch the ragged edge,
make each remaining stitch visible.

She slides the needle, a silver splinter
trailing a red tail,
through the intact stitches
gathering, anchoring, laying a fine lattice work
across the hole, weaving the sliver of silver
back and forth to repair.
She adds knots, fine, tight,
to prevent more unraveling.

In a swift movement
she brings the sock,
still swollen with the light bulb, to her mouth.
Her teeth flash as they
catch the red darning thread,
snap it cleanly.

She pulls out the light bulb,
folds the red sock with its mate,
grabs another damaged piece
from the mending pile.

Flip Side

round, black
slim, stack
seven singles
clickety-clack
cousin Arnold flips
forward and back
chooses the prize
to slide
over silver spindle
crook of thumb
pulls back
smooth brown
plastic lever
lowers stylus
onto shiny
flat sphere

ah'm all shook up
blares forth
the room explodes
into flared skirts
flying up and circling
girls' lithe waists
hips shimmy and tilt
knees bend and sway
bare feet point and prance
on polished brown
wood parquet

furniture
faces the wall
lined up
mute

and I, little sister
crawl onto
the displaced furniture
watching
feeling the beat
through the upholstery
quickening
to the deep voice
thrilling
to the *ah hums* and *o'yeahs*
peering
over high-backed armchairs
nose rubbing
against nubby fabric
dreaming
of my fingers
sliding
through the slick
black stack

and I will shake
my shoulders
throw my hips to one side
mouth the words
Ah'm all shook up
yeah yeah

Aunty Ruby's Eyes

are not like rubies
they crinkle through blue
cigarette smoke, her nose
wrinkles as she laughs
as the ice clinks
in her whiskey glass

Aunty Ruby's brown hair
once was golden
her plump waist
once was slim
her rosy calves
curve above her
black patent
sling-backs,
her hips shimmy
as she juggles
her smokes
her whisky

Aunty Ruby's gold earrings
swing, swing
her voice
crunches,
her laughter rings,
her accent, so English,
Hello Darling!
She flicks her wrist, her bracelets
cling, cling

Aunty Ruby flings open
her arms and sings
God Save the King

Hitch, or My Summer of Love

That was the summer
I hitched
a ride to Swaziland.

At the volunteer work-camp
poems of love
stitched
the blue sky.

I made my pitch
to be one of the bricklayers
but I'd never laid brick
before so instead my job
was to fill in the cracks
between the bricks
with floppy cement.

My work partner was a snitch.
She worked the other side of the wall
and reported if I left any fissures
between the bricks.

After three days, I was demoted to
the water bucket line.

I'd finally found my niche-
struggle uphill
weighed down by a full pail

then stroll back to the river to fish
love poems from muddy shallows.

Johannesburg

Jo'burg.
I am Jo'burg.
I am Jewish.
I am Jo'burg Jewish.

City of gold.
City of yellow. City of shine.
City of sulphureous mine dumps.
I am yellow. I am Jo'burg.

In the night you come, yellow
with your feet thudding,
past my window.
I am Jo'burg. I am yellow.

On hot days in the pool
rays of sun yellow my shoulders.
I am Jo'burg. I am saffron yellow. I am Jewish.

Yellow stars don't shine. Yellow patches
star the coats of my relatives in Eastern Europe.
Far away from Jo'burg.
Far away from Jo'burg Jewish.

In the day, Jo'burg, you come to the whites,
bearing gifts of gold, of jewels, gifts of clothes, perfume.

In the day, Jo'burg, you turn away
from the blacks. You unshine them.
They droop. They drop.
They yellow into red earth.

I am yours, Jo'burg. You are not mine.
I fled from your rocky hills, your buzzing hibiscus.
I could not unyellow my heart.
Not for me the heroic shine.

I am Jo'burg Jewish. I am yellow.

The Girl Who Raised Fantail Pigeons

~after Tess Gallagher's "The Woman Who Raised Goats"

In the walk-in cage of iron bars and chicken wire
you flutter from perch to perch.

You sidle up to each other, bob your heads,
coo like water emptying from a bottle.

Every day my parents leave the red-brick house,
backs straight, eyes blank, car piled with produce to sell.

But when I offer to help earn my keep
the uncles lean back against their velvet chairs,

inhale the smoke from their cigars,
half laugh, half cough, sip their whiskey.

No, no, you could be pretty too.
If only you put on some lipstick,

some make-up. If only you straightened
your hair. You'll see, some nice boy will want to take you home.

I turn back to the pigeons. Oh my dear ministers,
your eyes outlined in white, your tails fanned, you strut in the dirt.

I cover my head when I enter your cage.
Every day I drift further and further away

from the red brick house. Tomorrow I will leave
your cage door open.

Some of you will fly away.
Some will stay.

Tomatoes

You hang on a green
curling stalk
eating sunshine

casually lounge
on each other
at the market stall

occasionally dance
to the edge
of the counter

busting a samba move
at noon, afraid
to be left behind.

Sliced into luscious
thick discs
you hope to be placed

on a shield of
Mozzarella, topped
with a sprig of basil

surrounded
by gathered skirts of
black balsamic vinegar

and golden olive oil
on an oval porcelain platter
edged with red and gold

[. . .]

center piece of a patio table
covered by a red checkered cloth
on a warm summer night.

Tomatoes?
My Austrian lover calls you *paradise apples.*
He knows a thing or two about paradise.

"I'll Blame It on the Wind"

—Claudia Savage, "Thick in the Throat, Honey"

the mistral
that rushed over the Steppes
cold and piercing,
piled up in the Alps,
poured down the Rhone Valley,
surrounded and shook
the old farmhouse on the hill,
tested the blue shutters,
worked them back and forth
wood straining against metal locks.

I'll blame it on the sun

that golden heat that touched all things
revealed all flaws and
quiet   secret   beauties.
The warmth that sank
through the branches
of the old cherry tree
and dropped over us as we sat
around a stone table
in the morning.

I'll blame it on the fresh baguette

cracking as it gracefully surrendered
to our thumbs' soft pressure
receiving the creamy goat cheese
sliding off our knives
and the shining gem of sweetly tart grape jelly
glistening and floating
on its slippery, yellow bed.

[. . .]

I'll blame them all

for the urge to rise from my mattress
on the red tiled floor in the early morning
tiptoe barefoot down the still dark corridor
push past the wooden door's momentary catch
on its flaking plaster frame
slide into your bed
as you held up the blanket
letting me settle into its shadow
over your body.

Land and Body

-after Elizabeth Woody's "In Memory of
Crossing the Columbia"

My crib was pink wood
my blanket soft white
but my bed was inside
a long, swaying sling
moving from continent
to continent
rocked by the rhythms
of trains, steamships, and airplanes.

The rocky spine of the koppie
with its narrow, dusty, twisting paths
behind our house
called to me
but I could not stay.

Women in dark rooms
cold continents away
cooking, sewing, cleaning
gave me their dark eyes, their thin lips, their tight curling hair.
The broken threads of their lives
quivered in heat waves
rising off dusty paths, empty asphalt roads.
The ether of their lives
re-formed and settled in me.

Now, my back rests in the soft black loam
of the Willamette Valley.
My belly fills with sweet blueberries from Hillsboro
peaches from Dayton.
My skin blooms to the sun's rays.
My blood rushes with the grey sluice of rain.

[. . .]

Here I conceived and birthed a daughter.
She swam through my heart and my heritage.
She grew and left this green and cloudy place
but returns with the seasons for celebrations
Thanksgiving, New Years, Labor Day.
The past's tendrils twist
through me, curl through her,
hold us tight.

After "The Other Hours" by Li-Young Lee

When I look at the mountains
I see a lifetime over three continents
ending   and beginning   and ending

When I listen to the rain
thud on the tar-shingled roof
I hear the dryness of twisted paths
tamped down mud-hard
by bare feet

Is it someone inside me
who hears heavy drops
bursting on cracked swollen ground?

When I think about the flat lands
where I was born
where my father was born
did I ever really live there?

Who sees the lamplight?
Who remembers the father's bowed head
in the yellow circle of light?
His hand to his brow?

Who remembers the laughter
of the brothers, the uncles?

Who remembers the mothers
serving heaping plates of chicken
roasted with apricots and cloves?

Notes

"To Those Who Came Before Me"

> *Kichlach*: crackers made with egg, salt, and flour, rolled out flat and cut into large diamond shapes and sprinkled with sugar.

> *Kreplach*: boiled dumplings filled with meat and served in chicken broth.

"Early Spring 1913, Roskiskis Lithuania"

> Based on a story my mother told me about how when she was very ill as an infant her mother and grandmother changed her name to elude the angel of death.

"Winter 1919, Lithuania"

> Based on a family story about how my mother's sister saved the family silver from marauding soldiers after the Russian revolution.

"What She Told Her Family About Her New Life"

> For my grandmother, who emigrated from Eastern Europe to Southern Africa in her twenties.

"Descendants"

> For my grandfather, Avram (1884–1925)

"Dad & Ezra & the Cold War"

> The Cold War touched countries in Africa including the Congo, source of uranium and other precious metals. In

[. . .]

the 1950s, the USA and Russia fought a proxy war. Patrice Lumumba, who wanted to assert local control over the country's wealth was branded a communist. After he was elected, he was assassinated by Moise Tshombe and his troops, a group considered pro-Western.

"Inyanga"

Inyanga is a traditional healer of South Africa.

Machau is a fermented maize non-alcoholic drink from South-Africa.

Umqombothi is homemade beer.

Koppie is a low hill or ridge.

"Land and Body"

Koppie is a low hill or ridge.

Acknowledgments

Cirque Journal: "My Mother Remembers Learning Piano, Kopjes, South Africa 1925" as "Piano Lessons" (Vol.11, No. 2)

Clackamas Literary Review: "What She Told Her Family about Her New Life" (May 2020)

Generations (*Motherscope*, Issue #4, 2021): "To Those Who Came Before Me," "Early Spring 1913, Roskiskis Lithuania," and "Johannesburg Diamond"

Oyster River Pages: "Ritual" (2019)

Rain Magazine: "Flip Side" (2018), "Tomatoes" (2018), "Hitch, or my Summer of Love" (2019), and "Emma Mends the World" (2020)

The Timberline Review: "Winter 1919, Lithuania" (Spring 2020)

Willawaw Journal: "First Winter in Kopjes, South Africa" (Fall 2019), "Deschutes River Dream" (Spring 2020), "Winter Dream" (Fall 2020), and *"Yorzeit"* (Fall 2020)

VoiceCatcher: "I'll Blame It on the Wind" (Spring 2018), "Land and Body" (Spring 2018), "Aunty Ruby's Eyes" (Fall 2019), and "The Girl Who Raised Fantail Pigeons" (Fall 2019)

"South Africa, 1925: A Refugee from Lithuania Reflects on Her New Life" was an Honorable Mention in the *Members Only* category of the Oregon Poetry Association's Spring 2020 contest.

In Gratitude

I am deeply grateful to the following:

Paulann Petersen, whose poems wakened in me the idea of *embodied poetics*. She extended a generous and welcoming hand to me, a beginning poet.

Kim Stafford coaxed us workshop attendees to poetry so kindly. He encouraged us to listen, to see, to humbly accept, to recognize the gentle muse, to keep writing, to mend the world, to share beauty, to share our poems, to *deliver the mail.*

Claudia F. Saleeby Savage's vibrant, colorful, sensual voice will always have a special place in my heart. She is a teacher and poet extraordinaire, brilliant, funny, gentle. She encourages her pupils to push the envelope, persist, go deeper, find our obsessions, go there, keep writing there, read our work aloud.

Second Sunday Poetry Salonistas, particularly the core group of Suzy Harris, Kris Demian, Dale Champlin, Sheryl Chomak, Stephanie Skinner, and Betsy Tyghe, for monthly (or so) meetings to read and study women poets, to lift up women's poetic voices.

Suzy Harris, Ann Farley, Kris Demian, Dale Champlin, Sherri Hope Davis, the kindest, most supportive critique group, who read closely, provide constructive criticism and great suggestions.

Suzy Harris, my long-time writing partner. We took our first workshops together from Kim Stafford and Claudia Savage. We took our first tentative steps into poetry together, meeting weekly to generate work (bi-weekly by phone during the pandemic). We forayed into publication together and continue studying poets and craft. We are each other's fan club and staunch poetry ally.

[. . .]

My sister Flora Hoodin, for carefully reading this manuscript and providing gentle suggestions support and gracious acceptance.

My brother Aubrey Mendelow, for his steady interest and encouragement.

Simone Popperl, my daughter, and Sean Larabee, my son-in-law, for their love, interest, and support.

Franz Popperl, my husband and greatest fan, for much patient listening and unwavering support.

Praise for *A Nest in the Heart*

Depicting her Lithuanian Jewish ancestors, her childhood in Johannesburg, and her adult years in America's Pacific Northwest, Vivienne Popperl's poems speak to us from "inside/ a long, swaying sling/ moving from continent to continent." Having grown up "Jo'Burg Jewish" in South Africa, Popperl evolved a remarkable, compassionate awareness of the inhumanity created by both apartheid and anti-Semitism. Calling on striking imagery and rich musical devices, employing a vibrant flair for a poem's ability to convey whole histories in mere vignettes, she gives us a moving first collection that reaches—regardless of its vast geographic scope—"for bedrock with every step." *A Nest in the Heart* is an impressive debut.

—Paulann Petersen, Oregon Poet Laureate Emerita

In Vivienne Popperl's luminous book, *A Nest in the Heart*, she listens for the unknowable stories of her ancestors—refugees from Lithuania, farmers and women doctors in Apartheid South Africa, letters from the dead—to come back to herself. "She kept her nerve," Popperl says of her mother's story, "fierce brave heart." The same could be said for Popperl's collection. It takes courage to tell the truth of our families, grace to make them shine. "Poems of love/ stitched/ the blue sky" she says of her youth in Johannesburg. Thankfully, throughout *A Nest in the Heart*, they still do.

— Claudia F. Saleeby Savage, author of *Bruising Continents*

In her stunning first collection, *A Nest in the Heart*, poet Vivienne Popperl explores the vicissitudes of family with rare lyricism. From Avraham and Sorah down to Mathilda, the poet's mother, the poetic lines demark a compelling history and the redemption of faith.

[. . .]

Vivienne's ancestors wage war with a baby's illness, trick a Russian soldier, and emigrate from Lithuania to Kopjes, South Africa. These poems are redolent with sensory imagery. "I offer my grandfather lemons/ and strawberry jam for his tea." In the new land, children taunt one young mother's accent, but there is also time for piano lessons and games of hide and seek. One after another, family matriarchs adapt to their varied circumstances leading to Vivienne's mother graduating from Medical School in 1939.

So many of these poems read as love letters. In gorgeous and stunning language even the most mundane tasks, the darning of a sock, "She slides the needle, a silver splinter/ trailing a red tail," to a rhythmic Elvis singing *ah'm all shook up*—while Vivienne, the youngest sibling, breathlessly watches "flared skirts/ flying up and circling/ girls' lithe waists."

Young love blossoms in "I'll Blame It on the Wind," and the reader is soothed into the poet's forever home in the Willamette Valley. This fine collection sends shivers up my spine—what beautiful words and what generous sentiments. There are many astounding lines in every poem.

—Dale Champlin, author of *The Barbie Diaries*
and *Callie Comes of Age*

About the Author

Vivienne Popperl lives in Portland, Oregon. Her poems have appeared in *Clackamas Literary Review, Timberline Review, Cirque, Rain Magazine, The Poeming Pigeon,* and other publications. She won second place in the 2021 Kay Snow Award for Poetry by Willamette Writers. Her dream landscape is Provence, Southern France, but she considers the Pacific Northwest her home.

About The Poetry Box

The Poetry Box® is a boutique publishing company in Portland, Oregon, that provides a platform for both established and emerging poets to share their words with the world through beautiful printed books and chapbooks.

Feel free to visit the online bookstore (thePoetryBox.com), where you'll find more titles including:

The Catalog of Small Contentments by Carolyn Martin

Dear John— by Laura LeHew

A Shape of Sky by Cathy Cain

A Long, Wide Stretch of Calm by Melanie Green

Of the Forest by Linda Ferguson

Let's Hear It for the Horses by Tricia Knoll

Stronger Than the Current by Mark Thalman

Sophia & Mister Walter Whitman by Penelope Scambly Schott

The Widow at the Piano by Sue Fagalde Lick

What We Bring Home by Susan Coultrap McQuin

Beneath the Gravel Weight of Stars by Mimi German

Tell Her Yes by Ann Farley

and more . . .

9 781948 461993